D1312237

DEFENDING OUR NATION

RESCUING HOSTAGES:
THE FBI

Series Titles

DEFENDING OUR NATION

RESCUING HOSTAGES:
THE FBI

FOREWORD BY

MANNY GOMEZ, ESQ., SECURITY AND TERRORISM EXPERT

BY

BRENDA RALPH LEWIS

MASON CREST

Mason Crest
450 Parkway Drive, Suite D
Broomall, PA 19008
www.masoncrest.com

Printed and bound in the United States of America.
First printing
9 8 7 6 5 4 3 2 1

Series ISBN: 978-1-4222-3759-5
Hardcover ISBN: 978-1-4222-3770-0
ebook ISBN: 978-1-4222-8026-3

Library of Congress Cataloging-in-Publication Data

Names: Lewis, Brenda Ralph, author.
Title: Rescuing hostages : the FBI / foreword by Manny Gomez, Esq., Security
  and Terrorism Expert ; by Brenda Ralph Lewis.
Other titles: Hostage rescue with the FBI
Description: Broomall, Pennsylvania : Mason Crest, [2018] | Series: Defending our nation | Includes index.
Identifiers: LCCN 2016053124| ISBN 9781422237700 (hardback) | ISBN
  9781422237595 (series) | ISBN 9781422280263 (ebook)
Subjects: LCSH: United States. Federal Bureau of Investigation. Hostage Rescue Team--Juvenile literature. |
Hostages--Juvenile literature. | Rescues--Juvenile literature.
Classification: LCC HV8144.F43 L49 2018 | DDC 363.2/3--dc23
LC record available at https://lccn.loc.gov/2016053124

Developed and Produced by Print Matters Productions, Inc.
(www.printmattersinc.com)
Cover and Interior Design: Bill Madrid, Madrid Design
Additional Text: Kelly Kagamas Tomkies

CONTENTS

KEY ICONS TO LOOK FOR:

Words to understand: These words with their easy-to-understand definitions will increase the reader's understanding of the text while building vocabulary skills.

Sidebars: This boxed material within the main text allows readers to build knowledge, gain insights, explore possibilities, and broaden their perspectives by weaving together additional information to provide realistic and holistic perspectives.

Educational Videos: Readers can view videos by scanning our QR codes, providing them with additional educational content to supplement the text. Examples include news coverage, moments in history, speeches, iconic sports moments and much more!

Text-dependent questions: These questions send the reader back to the text for more careful attention to the evidence presented there.

Research projects: Readers are pointed toward areas of further inquiry connected to each chapter. Suggestions are provided for projects that encourage deeper research and analysis.

Series glossary of key terms: This back-of-the book glossary contains terminology used throughout this series. Words found here increase the reader's ability to read and comprehend higher-level books and articles in this field.

FOREWORD

VIGILANCE

We live in a world where we have to have a constant state of awareness—about our surroundings and who is around us. Law enforcement and the intelligence community cannot predict or stop the next terrorist attack alone. They need the citizenry of America, of the world, to act as a force multiplier in order to help deter, detect, and ultimately defeat a terrorist attack.

Technology is ever evolving and is a great weapon in the fight against terrorism. We have facial recognition, we have technology that is able to detect electronic communications through algorithms that may be related to terrorist activity—we also have drones that could spy on communities and bomb them without them ever knowing that a drone was there and with no cost of life to us.

But ultimately it's human intelligence and inside information that will help defeat a potential attack. It's people being aware of what's going on around them: if a family member, neighbor, coworker has suddenly changed in a manner where he or she is suddenly spouting violent anti-Western rhetoric or radical Islamic fundamentalism, those who notice it have a duty to report it to authorities so that they can do a proper investigation.

In turn, the trend since 9/11 has been for international communication as well as federal and local communication. Gone are the days when law enforcement or intelligence organizations kept information to themselves and didn't dare share it for fear that it might compromise the integrity of the information or for fear that the other organization would get equal credit. So the NYPD wouldn't tell anything to the FBI, the FBI wouldn't tell the CIA, and the CIA wouldn't tell the British counterintelligence agency, MI6, as an example. Improved as things are, we could do better.

We also have to improve global propaganda. Instead of dropping bombs, drop education on individuals who are even considering joining ISIS. Education is salvation. We have the greatest production means in the world through Hollywood and so on, so why don't we match ISIS materials? We tried it once but the government itself tried to produce it. This is something that should definitely be privatized. We also need to match the energy of cyber attackers—and we need savvy youth for that.

There are numerous ways that you could help in the fight against terror—joining law enforcement, the military, or not-for-profit organizations like the Peace Corps. If making the world a safer place appeals to you, draw on your particular strengths and put them to use where they are needed. But everybody should serve and be part of this global fight against terrorism in some small way. Certainly, everybody should be a part of the fight by simply being aware of their surroundings and knowing when something is not right and acting on that sense. In the investigation after most successful attacks, we know that somebody or some persons or people knew that there was something wrong with the person or persons who perpetrated the attack. Although it feels awkward to tell the authorities that you believe somebody is acting suspicious and may be a terrorist sympathizer or even a terrorist, we have a higher duty not only to society as a whole but to our family, friends, and ultimately ourselves to do something to ultimately stop the next attack.

It's not *if* there is going to be another attack, but where, when, and how. So being vigilant and being proactive are the orders of the day.

Manny Gomez, Esq.
President of MG Security Services,
Chairman of the National Law Enforcement Association,
former FBI Special Agent, U.S. Marine, and NYPD Sergeant

CHAPTER 1

TAKING HOSTAGES, PAST AND PRESENT

In order to successfully rescue a hostage without harm, officials must go through hours of training. Although they may not be able to reenact every part of a hostage situation, these training scenarios will prepare them for what may come.

To become a hostage is a terrifying experience. One moment you are leading an ordinary life, uninterrupted by dramatic events; the next, you are the prisoner of a desperado who is using you to make demands. And if these demands are not met, you may be killed. Suddenly, your life has changed, and you have no control over it. All you can do is wait and pray.

Now your life is in the hands of two groups of people: those who have taken you hostage and those who are trying to free you. The Federal Bureau of Investigation (FBI) has its own Hostage Rescue Team (HRT), whose members have been specially trained to free hostages unharmed.

The HRT was established in 1983 by Danny O. Coulson, an FBI operative who had spent over 30 years dealing with **terrorists**, assassins, and other criminals. The FBI had scored great successes against criminals, but in cases where hostages had been involved, too many of them had died. It was time, Coulson believed, to form a special organization dedicated to saving the lives of hostages.

The FBI Hostage Rescue Team.

Hostage taking is not a new development. The difference is that today it is much more violent and dangerous than it used to be; this is chiefly because of the modern guns, bombs, and other weapons that can be used in terrorist and hostage situations.

Words to Understand

Conquistador: A leader in the Spanish conquests of America, Mexico, and Peru in the 16th century.

Ransom: Money paid for the release of someone kidnapped or captured.

Terrorist: Using violent acts to frighten people to achieve a political goal.

Members of the FBI's Hostage Rescue Team.

In Ancient Times

In the second century BCE in the Middle East, the Syrians seized the relatives of community leaders as hostages in their fight against their Jewish neighbors. The idea was to make the Jews think twice about attacking the Syrian army: if they did so, then their relatives would be killed.

The army of ancient Rome did the same with the tribes they were fighting and sometimes made hostages of a chieftain's children to make sure he behaved himself. Sometimes, money was the motive for hostage taking. For example, in medieval times, important people like kings or nobles were often held as hostages in exchange for large **ransoms**. This was usually after they had been taken prisoner in a war; but as hostages they were well treated, with all the honor due to their high position.

Money and vengeance were the reasons behind the most famous act of hostage taking in English history: King Richard I, known as the Lionheart. In 1191, Richard was one of the leaders of the Third Crusade against the Muslims in the Holy Land. While in the Holy Land, it seems that Richard insulted another leader, Duke Leopold of Austria. Leopold vowed to get his revenge.

In 1192, Richard was in Vienna, Austria, on his way home to England when Duke Leopold captured and imprisoned him. The duke then demanded an enormous ransom of 150,000 marks (around U.S. $67,000) for Richard's release. Richard remained Leopold's prisoner and hostage for over a year, until February 1194—that was how long it took for the government in England to raise the ransom by taxing Richard's subjects.

The Conquistadors

Almost four centuries later, in what are now Central and South America, the Spanish

Richard Cœur de Lion and Saladin.

Richard I.
From the Statue on his Monument at Fontevrault.

King Richard I of England.

conquistadors found themselves facing danger. To protect themselves, they took hostages. The first of the conquistadors was Hernán Cortés, who invaded Aztec Mexico in 1519. By November, Cortés and his small army of only 550 Spaniards had reached Tenochtitlán, now Mexico City. They were greeted enthusiastically by the people of Tenochtitlán and their ruler, Montezuma, but not all Aztecs welcomed the Spanish intruders.

The Aztec priests in particular hated and feared them, believing that the Spaniards meant to destroy the Aztec religion and the Aztec empire with it. This is exactly what the Spaniards meant to do, but they were greatly outnumbered; the Aztecs could easily have killed all of them. So, to gain control over the Aztecs, Cortés decided to make Montezuma his hostage. The emperor was imprisoned in his palace and from then on, he was manipulated by Cortés and forced to obey his orders.

Illustrations portraying the conquest of Mexico by Hernán Cortés.

THE CONQUEST OF MEXICO BY HERNANDO CORTEZ. 17

FIRST VIEW OF THE MEXICAN CAPITAL.

THE CONQUEST OF MEXICO BY HERNANDO CORTEZ.

THE MEETING OF CORTEZ AND MONTEZUMA.

THE CONQUEST OF MEXICO BY HERNANDO CORTEZ. 21

THE BATTLE UPON THE CAUSEWAY.

Emperor Montezuma greeting the Spaniards.

The Aztec priests rebelled. Montezuma was killed, and the Spaniards were driven out of Tenochtitlán. However, they returned in 1521 to defeat the Aztecs and took over the Aztec empire.

In 1532, a second Spanish conquistador, Francisco Pizarro, was facing a similar situation in Tahuantinsuyu, the great Inca empire that covered present-day Peru, Bolivia, and Ecuador, as well as parts of Chile. Pizarro's army was even smaller than Cortés's—only 180 men. Soon after he arrived at the Inca town of Cajamarca, Pizarro took as his hostage the Inca ruler, Sapa Inca (Supreme Lord) Atahualpa. Just as Cortés had done 13 years earlier in Mexico, Pizarro was making sure that he and his army would be safe.

Atahualpa had extraordinary power over his Inca subjects: they believed he was a god and obeyed him without question. So when Atahualpa offered Pizarro a gigantic ransom for his freedom—a room full of gold, and two rooms of silver—the Incas obediently collected these precious metals from all over Tahuantinsuyu. Atahualpa now expected to be released. And Pizarro now realized just how powerful his hostage was; the Sapa Inca could order his people to do anything. What if he directed his subjects to kill all Spaniards? Pizarro could not afford to let Atahualpa go. Instead, he executed his hostage in 1533.

Inca Ruler Atahualpa.

No Negotiations

In the past, kings and rulers like Richard the Lionheart, Montezuma, and Atahualpa, and members of the aristocracy were the only people worth taking hostage. Who else had the money and power to pay big ransoms? Today, hostage taking is a different matter—and a much more dangerous one. Anyone, rich or poor, powerful or ordinary, can become a hostage. The hostage takers gamble that the hostages' governments will agree to any demands they make.

The state of Texas held Kiowa chief Set-Tainte, shown at left, captive—or hostage—until the Kiowa remained docile on their reservation lands to gain his release in 1873.

However, this is not always the case. The U.S. and British governments, for example, consistently refuse to negotiate with terrorists and hostage takers. If there are no negotiations, no demands will be met. This, of course, puts the hostages in great danger. The same is true for hostage rescuers. Somehow, they have to free hostages in situations in which the hostage takers are willing to use guns and other weapons to stop them. Sometimes, hostage takers are willing to blow up the sites where the hostages are being kept—whether buildings or aircraft. Sometimes, too, they will even kill themselves rather than let the rescuers succeed.

In short, hostage takers and hostage rescuers have goals that are directly opposite. They struggle against each other to get their own way and win, but they also have quite different views about the value of human life. Every living thing wants to survive, but hostage takers who are willing to kill themselves ignore this natural instinct. For the rescuers, on the other hand, the survival of the hostages always comes first.

This is why the task of hostage rescue is so difficult as well as dangerous. It is not enough for rescuers to have more or better weapons or more men and women than their opponents. They need patience, careful planning, and a great deal of courage to make sure that the hostage takers are defeated and that the hostages themselves survive. The hostage takers, on the other hand, are far more desperate and have much less to lose.

Rescue at Entebbe

The Israeli raid on Entebbe, Uganda, is widely recognized as the model of how to rescue hostages and defeat the plans of terrorist hostage takers.

On June 27, 1976, Air France Flight 139, from Athens, Greece, to Tel Aviv, Israel, was hijacked by seven terrorists in the name of the Palestine Liberation Organization (PLO). On board were 207 passengers. The pilot was ordered to fly to Uganda, whose ruler, Idi Amin, supported the PLO. The aircraft landed at Entebbe, near Lake Victoria. First, the terrorists separated the passengers. One hundred and six were either Israelis or Jews, and these people were put into the airport's Old Terminal building. The other 101, people of other nationalities, were released. Finally, the terrorists issued their demand: the release of 53 terrorists from prison. If this demand were not met, they would kill the passengers.

The families of the passengers wanted the Israeli government to agree to the terrorists' demands. It refused. Instead, it decided on a daring plan to rescue the hostages. Operation Thunderbolt was launched. First, the Israelis announced that they would negotiate with the terrorists at Entebbe. Previously, they had always refused to do this. Secretly, however, the Israelis prepared four large Hercules C130 transport aircraft to fly the rescuers to Entebbe, which lay 2,500 miles (4,025 km) away.

The Hercules aircraft landed at the airport at 11:01 P.M. on July 4, 1976. The Israelis went into action at once. First, they killed the Ugandan soldiers guarding the hostages. Next, they shouted to the hostages to lie flat on the floor. A fierce gun battle with the PLO followed. It lasted only three minutes. All seven terrorists were killed. The Israelis ordered the hostages onto the Hercules transports, and at 12:02 a.m. on July 5, just an hour after landing at Entebbe, the aircraft took off and flew the 2,500 miles back to Israel. Sadly, the Israeli commander, Colonel Jonathan Netanyahu, was killed in the last moments of the rescue.

Rescued Air France passengers leaving the belly of the airplane in 1976.

Long Ordeal in Tehran

President Jimmy Carter (right) disembarks a helicopter at Camp David to meet about the Iran hostage crisis with his vice president and secretarires of state and defense in November 1979.

U.S. hostages arrive at Rhein-Main U.S. Air Force base in Frankfurt, Germany, after their release from Iran, on January 21, 1981.

As brought to life for younger Americans in the movie *Argo*, 52 Americans spent 444 days as hostages in their former embassy following the radical student overthrow of imperial power in Iran in 1979. Aligned with religious clerics who later became very controlling, Iranian students detested their powerful leader and American ally, the shah. The hostage taking proved pivotal in American presidential politics; struggling domestically, President Jimmy Carter lost a landslide election to California Governor Ronald Reagan, on whose inauguration day the Iranians released the longheld U.S. hostages.

Text-Dependent Questions

1. What is the HRT and what is its role in the FBI?
2. Who was responsible for holding King Richard I hostage in 1191?
3. Which Spanish conquistador held Sapa Inca Atahualpa hostage in 1532?

Research Projects

1. Research the HRT. When is this team called in and what special skills do they have?
2. What Israeli officials planned the rescue of the hostages at Entebbe? Did what happened match their original plan?

CHAPTER 2

LEARNING TO BE A HOSTAGE RESCUER

A SWAT team trains to infiltrate a building.

When he first began considering what sort of men and women would make good agents for the FBI's Hostage Rescue Team, Danny Coulson knew straightaway the kind of people he was looking for—extraordinary people.

HRT agents must be able to act on their own, but also know how to work with other agents. There will be exciting jobs and dull jobs, but both kinds have to be done in the same way—well and thoroughly. Agents cannot be afraid to take risks, but at the same time, they cannot be hotheads craving excitement. A sense of humor is particularly important. Humor helps break tensions and keeps agents from getting uptight about the job. It also helps to calm nerves and bind the team together—and the team is the most important thing of all.

Tough Training

The first HRT **trainees** were a group of 50 men and 1 woman. Arriving at the training academy at Quantico, VA, they were also the first to discover that working for the HRT is very, very tough. For a start, they soon realized that agents must have strong hands, arms, and backs. To reach the sorts of places where their terrorist opponents might be holed up, agents may have to make great physical efforts—jumping, climbing, swimming, running, crawling, parachuting, or **abseiling** down ropes from helicopters.

Words to Understand

Abseiling: Also called rapelling, a controlled vertical descent using ropes.

Obstacle course: A series of objects that people or animals in a race have to jump or climb over, go around, go under, etc.

Trainee: Person who is being trained for a job.

HRT trainees must have no fear—especially of heights. Parachuting and hanging out of helicopters are something they may find themselves doing quite frequently.

However, just managing this is not enough; trainees must also arrive at the "battleground" ready and fit to fight their opponents. The first test is a 4-mile (6 km) run. Next, they climb 20-foot (6 m) ropes over and over again, and afterward do several push-ups and pull-ups in the academy's gym. If these hard exercises are a struggle for a trainee—no good. If they manage to complete the exercises, but become exhausted—also no good.

The ability to obey orders instantly and without question is also tested in the gym. To tell which of the first trainees had this ability, Coulson watched their faces as they received instructions from the physical trainer. If they looked as if they could not wait to get going and showed no fear or doubt—good. If they frowned or looked worried—no good.

Then comes training in the use of guns. All trainees are given .375 Magnum revolvers, but not to shoot at stationary targets. They must use their guns in training in the same way they will have to use them in a real situation, with terrorists shooting back at them. This means firing guns accurately while running.

In later training for full-scale antiterrorist missions, they use live ammunition. Some of the trainees act as hostages and are placed close to targets representing their terrorist captors.

HRT members must take part in antiterrorist training exercises. This antiterrorist exercise pitted police against the chemical biological warfare terrorists.

The trick is to shoot down the targets without harming the hostages. It is a test both for these hostages and for the men and women shooting the guns: they are, after all, shooting live bullets close to their friends and teammates.

Who Dares, Wins: Britain's Special Air Service

On April 30, 1980, six Arab terrorists forced their way into the Embassy of Iran in London, England. They took 26 hostages. Their demand was simple: their own independent state in southwest Iran in return for the hostages' lives. In the next six days, five hostages were released, another was executed, and two others were injured.

Television cameras were filming outside the embassy building when, suddenly, viewers heard a loud explosion from bomb charges placed against the windows. Next, eight soldiers abseiled down ropes from the roof and crashed through the windows. In the fight that followed, all but one of the terrorists were killed. The remaining 20 hostages were rescued. The rescuers belonged to a special group—the Special Air Service (SAS), whose motto is "Who Dares, Wins." The SAS are experts at moving silently, hiding where no one can see them, and taking their enemies by surprise. Today, about 200 applicants per year try to become one of this elite force, and only 20 pass and join the regiment.

The aftermath of the attack on the Iranian embassy in 1980.

Training also includes testing whether trainees suffer from aquaphobia—fear of water. The reason is simple: in action, agents might have to swim a river or rescue hostages from a boat. The test is designed to be as frightening as possible. A brick is thrown into a swimming pool. The trainees are blindfolded, then told to hold their noses and jump into the pool from a 15-foot (5 m) diving platform. Once in the water, they are not supposed to come to the surface to breathe, but have to stay under and find the brick.

HRT trainees can also not afford to suffer from acrophobia—a fear of heights. HRT agents might have to work at great heights, so their training includes a "confidence course" to test whether this might be a problem. This involves using a ladder to climb up five-story buildings. This ladder is unsteady and feels unsafe as it shakes and rolls. Before they start, the trainees are told that if they fall off, they will probably be killed. They are given the choice not to climb it, but if they fail to climb, that is the end of their chance to be chosen for the HRT.

LAW ENFORCEMENT
Crisis & Hostage
NEGOTIATION

Where?

53%
Private
Residence

21% Apt/condo
4% Mobile home
3% Hotel/motel

How Long?

35%
2-4 hrs

26% 0-2 hrs
19% 4-6 hrs
11% 6-9 hrs

Communication?

39%
Exisitng
Phone

31% Bullhorn
25% Voice from cover
22% Face to face

SUBJECT

91% Male
39% Married
60% White
20% Black
82% No injury
40% 35-40 yrs old
72% Weapon used
37% Handgun
30% Alcohol used
39% Has criminal history

96%
NON-HOSTAGE
situations

Hostage: A person being held involuntarily by another person as leverage to force fulfillment of demands on a 3rd party
Non-hostage: Emotionally driven situation with no substantive demands & the person does not need anything from the police

VICTIM

58% Female
50% White
34% No relationship
26% Family
25% Under 18yrs
80% No injury
14% injury
17% Victim positively
influenced subject
45% Not mistreated

Resolution

56% Negotiation/surrender
20% Tactical/intervention
12% Combination
8% Escape
3% Police withdraw

3rd Party Used

17% of incidents

71% Incident unplanned

Incidents with:

Injuries
97% None
2% Law enforcement
1% Bystanders
Death
99% None
Violence
30% Onset
11% During
62% Unknown
Violence Against
70% Unknown
18% Selected Hostage/victim
12% Law enforcement

The basic facts about hostage scenarios may surprise you.

Created by: Jeff Thompson | Research Fellow Columbia University Law School Data source: FBI/HOBAS. Data accessed 8.22.2013

In this exercise Hostage Rescue Team members practice working in a close-quarters scenario.

HRT Weapons and Equipment

The HRT uses the most up-to-date weapons and equipment in their vital work of saving the lives of hostages, including the following:

- Submachine guns: small, rapid-firing weapons
- Handguns: guns that can be fired using only one hand
- Rifles: guns fitted with sights and used by HRT snipers, who shoot from well-hidden places at single targets
- Machine pistols: small handguns that can be fired automatically
- Munitions: explosives that can blow open doors
- Chemical munitions: usually "tear gas," fired in containers from shotguns or launchers to disable terrorists; agents also wear gas masks so that they will not be affected by gas used by terrorists
- Sound and light devices: these produce a loud noise and bright flashes of light, which deafen and confuse terrorists
- Night-vision devices: night-vision goggles or attachments to guns, which have their own infrared illuminators that enable agents to see in the dark
- Body armor: a vest made of Kevlar or other material that can resist bullets
- Tools for entering buildings: a ram, to batter at the door; a pry bar, to open doors at the side; a sledge hammer, for breaking down obstacles; and a bolt cutter, to cut through bolts and locks on doors
- Microphones: small listening devices that enable agents to hear what's going on inside a building
- Video systems: small viewing devices that enable agents to see what's going on inside a building

Obstacles and Examinations

FBI trainees lose the chance to become HRT officers if they fail to pass the FBI's extremely tough **obstacle course**. This is similar to the U.S. Marine Corps's course, but has obstacles up to 6 inches (15 cm) higher. The FBI course begins with a huge leap up into the air to grab a parallel bar and get over it, and includes carrying another trainee over a distance of 60 yards (66 m)—rescue for the HRT does not mean rescuing hostages only, but also carrying injured teammates out of danger.

There are also examinations to pass. One of these involves being ordered out of bed in the middle of the night to watch a video showing a real-life fight against terrorists. They then have to write a report about it, the sort of report that would be written by an FBI agent. The idea of this examination is to test the trainees' powers of observation under difficult circumstances, when they are only half awake—how well did they observe the events on the video and how clearly did they remember it afterward?

HRT agents must be able to observe and notice small signs or changes in the way terrorists operate. To combat the hostage takers, they must know and understand the enemy. This could prevent agents from being taken by surprise by their opponents and help them improve their chances of rescuing hostages without suffering casualties themselves.

In 1983, the first year of the HRT, a total of 150 trainees went through what must be the toughest set of tests ever created. Only 50 of them, the very best in the group, were chosen to be members of the team. As of 2016, fewer than 300 individuals have been selected to be part of the HRT.

See how Hostage Rescue Teams train.

The Last Fight

The last part of a rescue operation often takes place in rooms where the hostages are being held. This is the most dangerous situation, with hostages, their captors, and their rescuers all together in a small space. So rescuers train hard to make sure that they get it right.

- Four rescuers, sometimes five, do the work of "clearing the room"—killing or capturing the hostage takers and rescuing the hostages.
- The point man goes in first, holding in one hand a mirror or other device to enable him to see if anyone is hiding around a corner; and in the other, a handgun to shoot the first hostage taker to threaten him.
- The first clearing man follows the point man and is armed with a submachine gun. He shoots at other hostage takers in the room.
- The team leader deals with any hostage takers still able to fight. Once the team leader is in control, the point man and clearing man can leave and move on to the next room.
- The second clearing man shoots off any locks or door hinges preventing the rescuers from reaching the hostage takers. He also supports the team leader in dealing with the hostage takers.
- The rear guard may use a ram to break down a door, and guards the rest of the rescue team as they clear the room.

This Los Angeles Police Department SWAT (special weapons and tactics) team breaches a room, in a training exercise focused on breach and clear tactics.

Text-Dependent Questions

1. What is the SAS and what is its role in Britain?
2. What is one physical test HRT trainees must pass?
3. How is the way HRT trainees are taught to shoot different than the way other law enforcement officers are taught?

Research Projects

1. Research the SAS. When is this team called in and what special skills do they have?
2. What is the application process for becoming part of the HRT? What minimum requirements must applicants possess to be considered?

CHAPTER 3

PREPARING TO RESCUE HOSTAGES

Using a team lift technique to enter a target building.

Gathering Information

You might not think so from the action movies you see, but rescuing hostages does not necessarily involve barging into buildings, firing guns, crashing cars, or making a lot of noise. In fact, hostage rescue is often a quiet and calm affair. What is needed is patience, because a lot of time can pass before the action itself begins; this waiting can even be a bit boring.

Before a rescue can begin, there is a lot the agents need to know, both about the hostages and about their captors: how many people are involved; what weapons are being used; and the site where they are holed up, including the layout and the best way to enter. Rescuers even have to know what the hostages are wearing, just in case the hostage takers exchange clothes with them. When the guns start firing, the rescuers do not want to find that they have hurt the wrong people.

Rescuers also have to survey the surroundings of the site where the hostages are held. The most helpful places for them are high ground or hills. This will give the rescuers better chances of observing the building. High ground is also a good hiding place for **snipers**. Specially trained to shoot quickly and accurately, snipers have the ability to shoot a hostage taker who has come out into the open accompanied by a hostage, without harming the hostage.

Close to some houses and buildings will be **gullies** or culverts. These are useful for hiding rescuers as they approach the building and let them come nearer than would be possible if the ground were flat and level. However, this advantage may also be apparent to the hostage takers

Words to Understand

Gully: Small trench worn into the earth by running water.

Sniper: Person shooting at someone from a hidden place.

Stake out: Observe an assigned location to gather information.

A sergeant watches the perimeter with his 50 caliber sniper rifle.

themselves: gullies and culverts also make good escape routes. The team must ensure that the hostage takers do not have the opportunity to leave the area with their hostages.

In any hostage-rescue situation, it is impossible to guarantee that no mistakes will be made. However, the more information the rescuers have, the better their chances of success. This information can come from various sources. Police or FBI records will show if the hostage takers have committed crimes in the past, particularly violent crimes. Do they have a history of mental illness or of taking drugs? The records of hospitals and clinics may provide clues. How old are they? If the hostage takers are young, they are more likely to be violent. Have they suffered a personal tragedy—perhaps divorce or a death in their family? If so, the hostage taking or other crimes of violence may occur on the anniversaries of such events.

Rescuers who have **staked out** a building with hostages inside can also tell a great deal simply by using a pair of binoculars. Hostage takers do not usually remain hidden inside a building for the whole time. To ensure that everyone is aware of the situation and of what they are demanding, they will appear with their hostages at windows or even at the door. The rescuers watching from outside can decide just how likely they are to be violent—do the hostage takers keep on making threats, holding a gun to a hostage's head and talking about killing the hostage?

A joint Delta Force, Army, and FBI sniper test.

Electronic Devices

More important information can be gained by using high-tech electronic devices. Many of these cannot be used from a distance, so rescuers must risk approaching the building to attach the devices to the walls, ventilation systems, or even the chimneys on the roof. Of course, all this must be done quietly and carefully to prevent the hostage takers from realizing what is happening.

A device often used is the endoscope—in effect, this is a TV on a tube that can be pushed through holes in walls. The rescuers are then able to watch the hostage takers inside. Microphones in the chimney can pick up what is being said, as can electronic stethoscopes, which are similar to the stethoscopes used by doctors to hear what is happening inside the body.

It is even possible for the rescuers to learn how the hostage takers are thinking. Do they keep on talking about dying? Do they sound or look as if they are nervous? Do they boast about how powerful they are or how many booby traps they have laid around the building? Do they threaten to kill any rescuer who dares to come too near? If the answer to these questions is yes, the rescuers know that the hostage takers are desperate, possibly suicidal, and certainly unpredictable. They may turn violent at any time, without warning, and kill their hostages and also, perhaps, themselves.

The Negotiators

All this information helps build up a picture of the type of people the rescuers are dealing with and how they should be approached. This is where the hostage-rescue negotiator comes in. Negotiating a way out of a hostage situation is a tricky business. The hostage takers must not be made angry or upset during negotiations. They must not feel that negotiators are bullying or criticizing them. Negotiators try to make them believe that they understand, and even sympathize with, whatever pressures have driven them to take hostages in the first place. So negotiators speak very calmly. If they are visible to the hostage takers, they must not make any suspicious movements—as if they are reaching for a gun, for instance. None of this, however, means that hostage takers are able to start thinking that they can have whatever they want: the negotiator must always be in control of the situation.

An FBI hostage negotiator speaking into a two-way radio.

256

FBI agents and local negotiators used this pipe to communicate with a hostage-taker who held a five-year-old captive in an underground bunker for almost a week in southeastern Alabama. The crisis ended with the child's safe rescue.

One way of achieving this is to keep the hostage takers talking, forcing them to concentrate on small, unimportant details. Suppose the hostage takers want a supply of coffee. The negotiator will prolong the conversation by asking what kind of coffee? Instant? Filter? Cappuccino? Espresso? With milk or without milk? With sugar or without sugar . . . and so on. The hostage takers may not care what kind of coffee they get, but by being made to talk about such trivial matters, they cannot be doing anything else in the meantime. And as long as the conversation continues, they cannot be thinking quite so much about their hostages.

How Not to Rescue Hostages

- May 14, 1974: Three Palestinian terrorists attacked a school in Ma'Alot, Israel, and took 100 students as hostages. Unfortunately, the hostage rescuers, an antiterrorist unit called Sayeret Mat'kal, did not have the right information about where the hostage takers were in the school building, and they waited too long to attack. As a result, 26 of the hostages were killed and another 60 badly injured.
- November 25, 1985: Egyptian hostage-rescue commandos, Force 777, made a disastrous attack on an Egypt Air plane that had been hijacked on the way from Athens, Greece, to the island of Malta. Everything went wrong. Force 777 used explosives to enter the plane, and once inside, they opened fire indiscriminately. In all, 57 passengers died.

Marines conduct hostage scenario training utilizing their personal protective equipment.

Know Your Enemy

Negotiators might also grant small concessions, perhaps agreeing to let food into the building. However, in exchange, they will want one or more hostages set free. If the hostage takers are hungry enough, they may agree, especially if they have several hostages and thus can spare a few without weakening their own position. This way, the HRT can reduce the number of hostages at risk.

If the electricity or water supplies have been turned off from outside the building, this can make things uncomfortable for everyone inside. Negotiators may be willing to restore these supplies—but only if more hostages are set free or their captors agree to let them talk to their worried relatives outside. Negotiators will not agree to any big demands, such as sending alcohol, drugs, or weapons into the building; any or all of these could make the situation much worse.

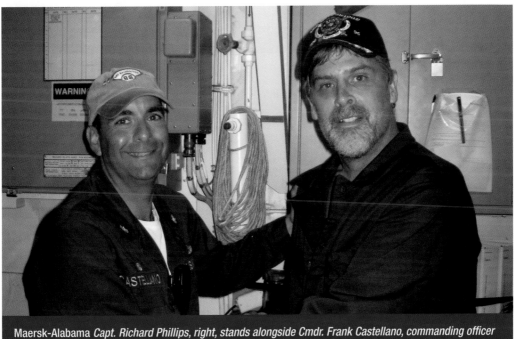

Maersk-Alabama *Capt. Richard Phillips, right, stands alongside Cmdr. Frank Castellano, commanding officer of USS Bainbridge after being rescued by U.S naval forces off the coast of Somalia. Philips was held hostage for four days by pirates.*

A sailor assigned to base security at Naval Air Station Whidbey Island covers the front entrance of a building during a hostage situation training exercise.

Whatever small concessions the negotiator makes, the basic situation remains the same. Most of the hostages and their captors are still holed up inside the building, and the rescuers are still surrounding it. But while the negotiator keeps the hostage takers occupied, the rescuers are waiting for the right moment to enter the house, rescue the hostages, and kill their captors or take them prisoner.

Of course, not all hostage-rescue plans go as smoothly as this, and sometimes rescuers have to use force to resolve the situation. Even so, the lives of many hostages have been saved by careful, patient rescue methods, and many hostage takers have been prevented from achieving their demands.

Interview with a former FBI negotiator.

Hostage Rescue Team operators participate in a training exercise. In a critical incident such as a terrorist attack or hostage situation, first responders are usually local and state-level law enforcement and might include SWAT teams and crisis negotiators. If a situation cannot be resolved at that level, federal assets such as the HRT may be called in.

Text-Dependent Questions

1. Name one piece of information a hostage rescue team member needs to know about a hostage situation before attempting rescue.
2. What is an endoscope and how do HRT team members use it?
3. What does a negotiator always need to be in control of?

Research Projects

1. Research to discover one mission in which HRT negotiated with hostage takers. What was the situation and how did negotiating help?
2. When is it OK to negotiate with hostage takers, and in what circumstances is it not recommended?

CHAPTER 4
THE SNIPERS

A camoflagued, masked sniper aiming at his target.

For most people, sharpshooting snipers belong to wars, killing enemies by shooting from hidden places and never missing their targets. It is true that, in war, snipers are the secret, silent killers, hidden away in trees or on high ground, behind bushes or walls. But snipers are also used in rescuing hostages, and they may sometimes kill hostage takers–and this is not their only role.

Because they are hidden, snipers can provide valuable information about the place where hostages are being held. They may be the first to realize that hostage takers are attempting an escape or to see where they have placed dangerous booby traps. The rest of the rescue team may not be able to see where an armed hostage taker is lying in wait for them–but the snipers can, and they are able to provide warning.

Hostage situations tend to take place in towns or other areas crowded with ordinary people. One of the sniper's tasks is to protect the hostages and also other members of the rescue team. When the rest of the team prepares to enter a building from one side, snipers will often fire their guns at the opposite side. This is known as creating a **diversion**. Hostage takers, hearing bullets hitting the outside wall, are made to think that the attack is coming from that direction.

On those occasions when a sniper has to kill, it is usually because the hostages or the rescue team are in danger. For example, a hostage taker may force a hostage to walk in front, as a shield against being attacked. What the sniper must do is wait for a chance to shoot the hostage taker, but not the hostage.

Words to Understand

Diversion: Something that takes attention away from what is happening.

Duct: Pipe or tube through which to run air, water, or electric power lines.

Reconnaissance: Personnel sent out to a specific location to gain information prior to a mission or plan.

What Qualities Do Snipers Have?

Snipers are very special people. First, they have to be physically strong: snipers often have to climb up trees or hills to get into position at the scene of hostage taking. They must also be very patient, because they have to wait for the best chance to hit their targets: more often than not, the best chance comes only after some time. Snipers cannot afford to be nervous, and they must never hesitate. They must always act as soon as they see their opportunity, and since this is usually an opportunity to kill, they must do it without thinking twice about it.

Snipers are often called "crack shots," which means that they are very accurate and know exactly when and where to fire their guns. However, they need more than a firm, steady hand, good eyesight, and the best telescopic sights for their rifles. Hostage rescues can take place in all sorts of weather conditions—rain, wind, even snow and ice. None of this should make any difference to the sniper's expertise. They must be able to calculate how to shoot accurately even in heavy rain or when the wind is blowing hard. Most often, snipers will have to shoot at moving targets. Hostage takers are not going to stand still or put themselves in a dangerous position, thus making it easier for snipers to get them in their sights. They will probably be on the move all the time.

Snipers may move to rooftops to get a better view of their targets.

Snipers also have to be adaptable, able to shoot from various positions. Firing from a rooftop, for instance, is quite different from hiding in a tree or inside a building and firing from there. Because of this, snipers practice using their guns in all the situations that might arise when there are hostages to be rescued.

"Traffic Lights" in Hostage Rescue

It is not always possible for the rescue teams to talk to snipers while a hostage rescue is ongoing. For this reason, many of these teams use traffic light colors as a code:

- Red light: Do not shoot.
- Yellow light: Shoot, but only if it means saving a life; the yellow light tends to be used when no hostages have been killed or injured.
- Green light: Shoot as soon as the hostage takers are lined up, in sight; the green light tends to be used when hostage takers have already killed or injured some of their hostages.

In addition, snipers have to be able to think and act quickly. Sometimes, there will be no time to make careful preparations. In such cases, they must select their targets, work out the range or distance between themselves and the targets, and know instantly what ammunition they must use—all in a few seconds. If snipers cannot work this fast, the chance to stop or kill a hostage taker and rescue a hostage may be lost.

The first thing to do is to become familiar with the area they have to cover and make sure they know its features—trees, hills, telegraph poles, even mail boxes. Snipers cannot afford to

An M-40 sniper scope mounted on a Remington Model 700 rifle.

overlook even the smallest detail. Anything and everything can be important. Before snipers can get into the right position, they have to do a lot of homework. Using binoculars or the scope on their rifles, which makes their targets look bigger, they must make a thorough reconnaissance of the area where the hostages are being held and of the surrounding areas.

The Sniper's Hide

The place where snipers conceal themselves is known as a hide. In a town or city, the best hide is usually inside an office or an apartment, preferably in a high-rise block on the opposite side of a street to the building where a hostage incident has occurred. The snipers can then choose which floor gives them the best advantage; if possible, they will choose a higher position, which lets them look down on the hostage takers and their hostages.

The Importance of Camouflage

Another important skill for snipers is an understanding of camouflage. Camouflage comes from the French *camoufler*, meaning "to disguise." If snipers take a position high in a tree, for example, they must disguise themselves so that they become part of the tree. By hanging twigs and leaves on clothing or helmets, or wearing clothes that have wavy green and brown patterns, the snipers will blend in with their surroundings. Other hostage rescuers use camouflage, of course, but it is especially important for snipers.

Buildings like these also offer snipers a lot of protection. If the building has many windows, all will be opened so that the hostage taker cannot guess which window the sniper is using. Snipers will also conceal themselves behind the curtains at a window.

Window frames and windowsills in city buildings can, of course, be dusty. When snipers fire their guns, the dust can be disturbed. This gives their position away and may also interfere with the telescopic sights on their guns. To prevent this from happening, a damp cloth is often placed under the muzzle of a sniper's gun.

Roofs make less-than-satisfactory hides for snipers. For a start, they are out in the open, at the mercy of the weather. Second, snipers dare not raise their head or their shoulders too

Royal Marines snipers have camouflaged themselves to better blend in to their surroundings.

high above the roof, because then they can be seen, silhouetted against the sky. On a roof, snipers always have to fire downward, at an angle, and this may not help them to be absolutely accurate with their shots.

There is a way around these problems, however. Many roofs have "boxes" that contain the **ducts** for air conditioning or central heating. Snipers may, therefore, make their own box out of cardboard, painting it to look like the other rooftop boxes.

The Art of Reconnaissance

"Reconnaissance" comes from the Old French word *reconnoistre*, which means "to recognize." **Reconnaissance** will also reveal whether there are any obstacles, like gates or small buildings, that might interfere with their line of fire. Snipers may not be able to avoid these obstacles altogether, but they can at least take this into consideration when choosing their position.

Reconnaissance is important, too, in helping to spot a position that is closest to the target. Of course, events do not always go according to plan, so snipers will be careful to choose two or three positions. In some situations, the sniper may use any or all of the chosen positions.

Suppose a sniper is seen by the hostage takers during the course of negotiations. They could take advantage of this by demanding that the sniper be removed. The negotiator agrees, the sniper moves, and the hostage takers think they have scored a victory. But what has actually happened is that the sniper has simply moved to another place, and the hostage takers are still within range of his rifle. The snipers may themselves choose to move, particularly if a shot has been fired, thus giving away their position. Staying where they are might mean risking death or injury if the hostage takers decide to open fire on this known position.

An officer conducts surveillance after dark from an unmarked vehicle during an operation shared by local law enforcement and the FBI.

Snipers often work with observers, who provide important backup. Observers help in reconnoitering the area. If a stakeout continues for a long time, observers will give the snipers a rest by taking over their rifles for a while. At other times, while the sniper is occupied, their observers are free to communicate with the rest of the rescue team and let them know the situation. The observer also has the job of defending the sniper's position, if necessary, and making sure that the position is safe and secure.

Keeping a Record

It may also be the job of the observer to log, or record, a hostage-taking incident. A log has at least two important purposes. First of all, what happens in one incident, including what action the snipers take, can provide valuable information for use in other hostage situations. Second, after an incident is over, there may be an official enquiry; the observer's log will provide evidence for that enquiry.

An FBI Evidence Response Team truck is parked at the scene of an attack two days earlier.

The log may also be used as evidence if hostage takers are captured and are later put on trial. Anyone who takes hostages always attracts a lot of anger from ordinary people, especially when young children have been made hostages. The terror of it is always much worse for these youngsters, who cannot understand what is happening but know that, whatever it is, it is dangerous.

A group of Evidence Response Team members walk in a field searching for evidence.

However, a court of law can never afford to be guided by anger or disgust or any other emotion. What counts in a court of law is the evidence, and only the evidence. The log kept at hostage rescue incidents provides some of the evidence that can prove whether hostage takers on trial are guilty or not guilty. Without it, there can be no trial. The hostage takers may walk free, perhaps to take more hostages and frighten more innocent people in the future.

Text-Dependent Questions

1. Name one of the primary tasks of a sniper on an HRT team.
2. Name one characteristic or quality a sniper on an HRT team must possess.
3. What does a yellow light mean during an HRT mission?

Research Projects

1. In addition to the traffic light system, what are other ways HRT members communicate with one another?
2. How often are snipers used in HRT missions? How much does the success of the mission depend on them?

CHAPTER 5

SHIPS AT SEA

In some instances, helicopters are necessary when assisting ships at sea. Here, a rescue operation team is being lowered onto a ship in need of assistance.

A ship at sea is like a world on its own. With its own stores of food and supplies, it can move anywhere across Earth's seas and oceans. If terrorists attempt to hijack a ship at sea, it is likely that they will make the passengers and crew their hostages.

Moreover, it is likely to be some time before the rescue teams can reach the scene. This leaves the terrorists free to secure the ship and assert their control, robbing the passengers, perhaps even killing some.

If the hijacked ship is a cruise liner, there are usually hundreds of passengers on board who will become hostages for the terrorists. By contrast, a trading ship or oil tanker, with only the crews on board, will mean fewer hostages. Even so, there are serious dangers. An oil tanker damaged in a terrorist attack might leak oil into the sea; or the hostage takers may deliberately leak the oil, using the threat of pollution to reinforce their demands. The marine life in the nearby waters can be poisoned and killed, while the beaches and shorelines and the birds who live on them can be covered in a sticky black mess as the oil drifts in—and birds covered in oil die very easily. Either way, the environmental damage may be considerable.

Gathering Information

Whatever type of ship is **hijacked** at sea, the rescuers must first gather as much information about it as possible. The shipping company that owns the ship can answer several important questions. How high up are the decks? Where are the stairways and the passageways or corridors? What sort of lighting system does the ship have? Does the ship have any ladders or ropes

Words to Understand

Hijack: To take control of an airplane or ship by force.

Bogus: False.

Buoyancy: Ability of an object to float in water or air.

along the side of the hull? (These could help the rescuers climb on board.) Do the hatches and portholes open inward or outward, and where are they located? How thick are the windows, and what type of glass are they made of? The rescuers may have to smash the glass, and they need to know how easy or difficult this is likely to be.

Once they have boarded a hijacked ship, the rescuers will probably have to break down parts of the bulkheads, the partitions between various sections inside. What are these bulkheads made of–steel, aluminum, or some other material? This will determine the type of equipment the rescuers use.

The Pascal Paoli was occupied by the Corsican trade union STC in 2005. Here, the GIGN (Groupe d'intervention de la Gendarmerie nationale), a rescue team, is boarding the ship.

A Turkish commando dons a bomb suit aboard the aircraft carrier USS George H.W. Bush during a joint exercise.

Getting a rescue team onto a hijacked ship—known as insertion—can be difficult, regardless if the ship is under way (moving over the sea) or riding at anchor (stationary). Rescuers climbing up the ship's side from below are at risk from terrorists above them on the deck. Firing guns downward is much easier than firing upward, particularly when hanging on a rope or ladder with only one hand free for defense. The goal, then, is to insert the team without the terrorists realizing until it's too late.

Usually, rescuers choose the stern of the ship as the place to board. Their intention is to surprise the terrorists by acting as quickly and as silently as possible. There are one or two tricks that can help. The small, fast boat carrying the rescue team can appear to have fishermen on board. These are, of course, rescuers in disguise, but the terrorists are not to know that and are unlikely to think that these "fishermen" are any danger. After all, fishing boats are a common sight at sea—sometimes quite far out to sea, in fact.

The Tools of Hostage Rescue

Teams rescuing hostages and dealing with terrorists on board a hijacked ship need special equipment that includes the following:

- Buoyancy panels: The SEAL units of the U.S. Navy wear special vests with buoyancy panels that enable the heavy weapons and equipment they carry to float in the water.
- Padded ladders: Ladders are padded so that they do not make a noise when placed against the sides of the ship.
- Slings for carrying weapons: Rescuers climbing on board a ship need both hands free, so they carry their guns and other weapons in slings.
- Night-vision equipment: At night, it is particularly dark at sea, especially if the electricity system on a ship has been cut off; the answer to this problem is night-vision equipment. One piece of equipment is a pair of goggles with its own infrared illuminating system; another is night-vision equipment mounted on a rifle. These night-vision optics, as they are called, make the greatest possible use of low light, like starlight or the light of the moon, and enable rescuers to see in the dark.

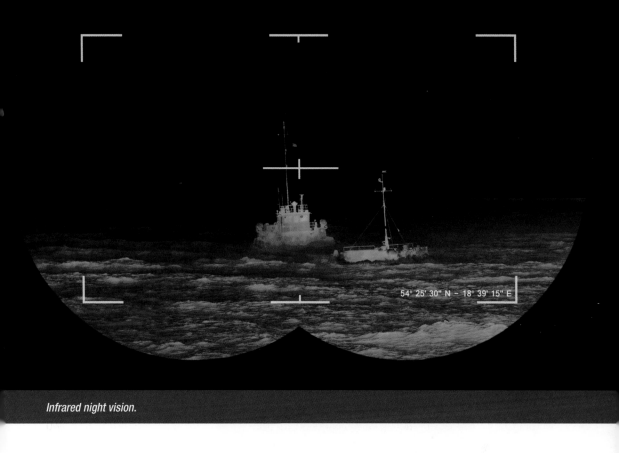

Infrared night vision.

The **bogus** fishermen may wave, shout, ask for help, perhaps give warnings of approaching storms—anything and everything that can distract or catch the terrorists' attention and prevent them from knowing the ship is being boarded.

Fake Holidaymakers

Another way of distracting the terrorists is for members of the rescue team to pretend they are passengers taking a day trip out at sea from a holiday resort on a nearby coast. They will dress in beach clothes to look perfectly harmless. Some of the women among the "holidaymakers" have a special trick they can play. They dress up in skimpy bikinis in order to attract the attention of the hostage takers. And while they are eyeing the women and flirting with them, they are not thinking about anything else. This gives the rescuers a good chance of getting on board the hijacked ship without being noticed. This gives them the advantage of surprise. By the time the hostage takers realize the deception, they are under attack.

Swimmers in Rescue Work

The swimmers and divers in a hostage rescue team do not usually take part in assaults on hijacked ships. Even so, their role is important. Moving silently and unseen through the water around the ship, swimmers and divers can gather information about the ship and take pictures of it with underwater video and other cameras.

Divers have to be careful not to give themselves away, so they use special breathing apparatus that does not let bubbles rise to the surface while they are underwater. It takes a lot of courage to be a diver in hostage rescue work. The French counterterrorist unit *Groupe d'Intervention Gendarmerie Nationale* (GIGN) tests its divers with a frightening ordeal. They must dive into the River Seine, which runs through Paris, and lie on the bottom for long periods of time.

This Navy SEAL diver stays undetected, underwater, while being transported from submarine to enemy targets.

Using Helicopters

Rescuers can also be dropped by helicopter. However, this is a noisier method and will attract a lot of attention. To make sure they do not give the game away too soon, the helicopters approach the ship flying very low over the sea. At the right moment, the helicopter pilot then pulls back on the controls and the helicopter rises up into the sky, over the stern.

Suddenly, rescuers are abseiling fast down ropes, out of the helicopter and directly onto the deck. Before they reach the deck, they may be easy targets for the terrorists, who can pick them off with gunfire. However, the helicopter can give them some protection with covering fire aimed down at the terrorists.

U.S. Navy SEALs are lowered by helicopter onto a hostile ship.

The Hijack of the *Achille Lauro*

Not all hostage-taking incidents end with the death or punishment of the terrorists involved. One such incident was the hijacking of the Italian cruise liner, the *Achille Lauro*, on October 7, 1985.

The liner was sailing along the Egyptian coast from Alexandria to Port Said when it was hijacked by five terrorists of the Palestine Liberation Front (PLF). There were 454 passengers and crew on board. The terrorists demanded that 50 PLF men held prisoner in Israel be freed, or the ship would be blown up. One of the 19 American passengers, a disabled man called Leon Klinghoffer, argued with the terrorists. They killed him and threw his body overboard, still strapped to his wheelchair.

President Ronald Reagan discusses the Achille Lauro *hijacking with his National Security Advisor Robert McFarlane.*

This produced shock and outrage worldwide, but particularly in the United States. Within a few hours, commandos of the U.S. Navy SEALs arrived at Akrotiri on the Mediterranean island of Cyprus and made preparations to rescue the hostages. However, by the time they were ready, on October 9, the terrorists were no longer on board the ship. They had sailed the *Achille Lauro* to Port Said, where they made new demands. They would surrender, they said, if they were not prosecuted and were released into PLF custody.

The Egyptian government agreed and sent an aircraft to Port Said to fly the terrorists to safety in Tunisia, North Africa. The U.S. government was furious and tried to stop their escape. Two U.S. Navy fighters were sent to force the Egyptian plane to land in Sicily, an island off the southwest coast of Italy.

In Sicily, the terrorists were arrested by the carabinieri, the Italian police. Later, the Italian government let two of them and their leader, Mohamed Abbas, go free. The other two were put on trial and sent to prison.

The rescue team's best defense, however, is speed. The U.S. Navy's counterterrorist unit, SEAL Team 6, is expert in the use of helicopters in rescue work. A helicopter hovering 60 feet (18 m) above the ship can land six men down fast ropes within four seconds, even though the deck may be moving up and down with the motion of the sea. Speed is also important for the safety of the helicopter itself. To guard against being shot down, the pilot flies away quickly once the rescue team is safely on board.

Now that the rescuers are on board, they must move fast to find the hostages. This is no easy task. The inside of a ship is a mass of stairways, passages, and cabins. All of them have to be searched, and any of them may contain one or more terrorists willing to fight to the death. Some of the passageways are very narrow, so the rescuers have to bend low, or even crawl along the floor.

As always, the first thing to be done is to get the hostages to a place of safety elsewhere on the ship. As for the terrorists, the ship they hijacked is now a trap, with few ways of escaping. Sometimes, it is possible for them to negotiate for their freedom. But in most situations, there is nowhere to go. Either they surrender or they are killed by the security forces.

Text-Dependent Questions

1. What is the first step in the rescue process when a ship has been hijacked?
2. What is especially challenging when it comes to rescuing a hijacked ship?
3. What is one distraction HRT uses to get some of its team onboard a hijacked ship?

Research Projects

1. How many HRT members typically respond to an HRT mission? What determines the number of members needed?
2. How many HRT missions have been to recover hijacked ships? How successful were these missions?

CHAPTER 6

HOSTAGES ON AIRCRAFT

A deflated evacuation slide on the back of an A320 Airbus.

n 1968, defeating terrorists and rescuing hostages gained a new urgency. On July 23 of that year, a Boeing 707 airliner belonging to El Al, the Israeli national airline, was hijacked by three members of the Popular Front for the Liberation of Palestine (PFLP).

The 32 passengers on board became hostages. The airliner was scheduled to fly from Tel Aviv, Israel, to Rome, Italy. However, the pilot was forced to fly to Algiers, Algeria. Once there, the hijackers refused to release their hostages until they were guaranteed that they would not be punished or imprisoned for their crime. After five weeks, all the hostages were released, and the hijackers escaped. The incident made front-page news around the world. However, it was not the first time an aircraft had been hijacked. The first known airliner hijacking occurred in Peru. On February 21, 1931, an American pilot, Byron Rickards, was taken hostage, then held for 10 days by revolutionaries who wanted to use his aircraft for transport.

After World War II ended, several planes were hijacked by refugees whose lives were in danger because they were opposed to the new governments, usually Communist governments, that had come to power in their countries. Hijacking a plane and getting it to fly where they wanted was their way of escaping.

Air Piracy

What made the El Al incident of 1968 different was not the hijacking itself but the fact that it was done for political reasons. The PFLP, which had been formed only

Words to Understand

Air marshal: Trained federal security personnel who ride public airplanes in plainclothes to protect passengers from hijacking.

Fuselage: The main body of an aircraft.

Jumbo jets: Class of wide-body commercial and cargo airplanes.

seven months earlier, wanted to publicize their quarrel with Israel over the treatment of Palestinian Arabs. The PFLP and its activities have been known worldwide ever since.

This was the first of many PFLP hijackings. Even worse, it was also the start of an enormous increase in this type of crime, which became known as air piracy. In 1969, there were 82 aircraft hijackings, more than twice the number that had occurred in the previous 20 years. Between 1967 and 1976, some 385 aircraft were hijacked. Over the next 10 years, the situation seemed to improve. Hijackings dropped to 300, and between 1987 and 1996, they dropped even lower, to 212. After September 11, 2001, hijackings became fewer in number, thanks to increased airport security. However, the 2010s has still seen a half-dozen hijackings. One of the more recent hijackings occurred on March 24, 2015, when a Germanwings flight was hijacked by the copilot. He crashed the plane into the Alps.

Special Dangers

El Al, the Israeli airline, was in a particularly dangerous position, since the quarrel with the Palestinians continued for many years–and is still not at an end. El Al aircraft often carried Jewish passengers visiting Israel, or Israeli citizens returning home from abroad. El Al, therefore, continued to be a target for terrorists. Because of this, El Al is allowed even today to park its aircraft in special areas at airports around the world. These areas are well away from any place where a terrorist might be able to approach and get on board. No other airline has felt the need to take such precautions, but all have increased their security. Before passengers are allowed to board aircraft, they are now searched for weapons. They must walk through metal detectors and body scanners connected with videos that show security personnel any items a person is carrying that may be a weapon. In addition, there are limits to carry-on bags and their size, as well as what is allowed to be carried on inside the bags.

Attorney General Robert Kennedy swears in the first Sky Marshals in 1961.

Some airlines, like El Al, even put armed **air marshals** on board, disguised as passengers. These are very much like the guards who used to "ride shotgun" on mail and passenger coaches in the days of the Wild West in the United States. The air marshals carry special guns to deal with hijackers while the aircraft is still in flight. It is dangerous to fire guns inside an aircraft because the bullets can puncture the aircraft's outer "skin" and cause the aircraft cabin to explode or crash. Special ammunition is therefore used to avoid this dangerous hazard.

These measures all help reduce the problem of aircraft hijacking, but do not get rid of it completely. Determined hijackers manage to get on board aircraft just the same, and the taking of hostages continues today. As a result, special teams of rescuers have now been trained to assault hijacked airliners, releasing the hostages and dealing with the hijackers. They have only one opportunity–after the aircraft has landed at an airport. This airport is either the one chosen by the hijackers or an airport where they have been forced to land by a shortage of fuel.

Rescuing hostages from hijacked aircraft has its own special problems. One of them is that the aircraft interiors are small, narrow, and crowded. It can be difficult to tell who is a hostage

A Rescue That Succeeded

In 1977, Arab hijackers, led by the notorious terrorist Zohair Youssef Akache, united with the German terrorist Baader-Meinhoff gang in an attempt to secure the release of gang members from prison. On October 13, four Arabs hijacked a Boeing 737 jet belonging to Lufthansa, the West German airline. It was flying 86 passengers to Germany from Palma, in the Balearic Islands (in the Mediterranean Sea).

The flight was diverted to Rome, where Akache demanded that the aircraft be refueled or he would blow it up. He made the same threat after the aircraft landed in Cyprus. On both occasions, the fuel was provided. Akache then forced the pilot to fly to Mogadishu, the capital of Somalia. There, a team of rescuers was waiting.

The aircraft was assaulted on the runway by 22 rescuers: 20 of them came from the Grenzschutzgruppe 9 (GSG-9), the German counterterrorist unit, and two were members of the British Special Air Service (SAS). The SAS carried "stun" grenades, which they threw against the front of the aircraft. The four hijackers, thinking the rescue attempt was going to take place there, rushed forward to stop it, only to find that this "attack" was a trick. The rescuers entered the plane behind them and rescued the hostages, killing or capturing the hijackers.

and who is a hijacker. In addition, there is always the danger that an armed rescue can result in a fire on board the aircraft. This, of course, puts the hostages at great risk, which is why flammable gases are not normally used in rescues from hijacked aircraft.

Another problem for rescuers is that the many planes flying the world's air routes are of different designs. For example, not all planes have the same type of doors. Rescue teams must know the type of door and how it opens if they are going to get into the aircraft quickly. **Jumbo jets**, such as the Boeing 747 or the Douglas DC-10, have doors with hinges on one side that swing out to let passengers get on and off the plane. The doors on the Boeing 767, however, are electronically operated and swing upward. The smaller Boeing 727 has a door at the back of the aircraft; passengers get on and off by means of a built-in stairway. These differences mean that rescue teams have to practice getting into every kind of aircraft used by the major airlines.

Sometimes, a rescue team will decide to get into an aircraft by using the emergency doors placed along the **fuselage** above the wings. The best chance of success lies with using team members who are not too large and heavy; they are less likely to make the wing move or rock, and thus have a better chance of creeping along it to the emergency doors and taking the hijackers by surprise before they know what is happening.

Why Hijack Aircraft?

There are several reasons why aircraft have proved to be useful targets for terrorists.

- Airlines and their aircraft are symbols of the country to which they belong. Indeed, airlines are often government owned, and as such the aircraft are their countries' "national flag carriers." Terrorists who have a quarrel with, say, the United States, Israel, or France–all of them countries whose aircraft have been hijacked–believe they are striking a blow against the country itself.
- A hijacking, like all acts of terrorism, makes headlines across the world. It is an effective way to promote a cause.
- An aircraft in flight has a ready-made collection of hostages–the passengers and crew, none of whom can escape from a craft 30,000 feet (9,144 m) or more up in the air.
- In addition, aircraft can go anywhere in the world as long as they have enough fuel. Usually, the countries to which they want to fly are likely to be friendly toward them.
- The hijackers can threaten to kill their hostages unless their demands are met and they are given the fuel they need. This is the ultimate weapon available to the hijackers.

Stuttgart Intercon

The freed hostages of the 1977 hijacking.

Another way to get into an aircraft is by using ladders. Of course, doors are at different heights on different aircraft; the ladders must be the right length. They must also be strong enough to let the rescuers climb them while carrying heavy equipment and weapons. However, although rescue teams are well equipped and thoroughly practiced at getting hostages out of hijacked aircraft, they do not always manage. Sadly, it often happens that hostages are killed or injured during a rescue.

Hostage rescue is a risky business. No one can ever be sure of success because violence is usually involved and cannot be easily controlled–nervous hijackers can become violent all too easily. So a rescue team faces a difficult decision: will the hostages be in greater danger if it does not attempt a rescue, or if it does? As a rule, rescues take place only if the hijackers are so violent that the hostages are bound to be killed or injured, and rescue, however dangerous, is their only chance to survive.

A sign in an African airport warning about hijacking.

Antiterrorist and Hostage-Rescue Teams of the World

Terrorism and hostage taking are problems all over the world. Here are some of the organizations whose job it is to fight against them.

The U.S. FBI SWAT teams and France's GIGN are just two groups that help in saving citizens.

Australia:
Australian Special Air Service Regiment

Canada:
Joint Task Force 2

Great Britain:
Special Air Service (SAS)
Special Boat Service (SBS)
Royal Marines

France:
Groupe d'intervention Gendarmerie
Nationale (GIGN)

Germany:
Grenzschutzgruppe 9 (GSG-9)
Kommando Spezialkraefte (KSK)

India:
National Security Guards (NSG)

Indonesia:
Kopassus

Israel:
Unit 269 (Sayeret Mat'kal or
General Staff Reconnaissance)
D4 (Flotilla 13, The Batmen)

Italy:
Divisione Operazioni Speciale
(Special Operations Division–NOCS)
Gruppo Intervento Speciale
(Special Intervention Group–GIS)

Russia:
Omon (The Black Berets)
Alpha Group A (AL'FA)
Spetzgruppa Vympel (Special
Opérations Unit–VYMPEL)

United States:
FBI Hostage Rescue Team (HRT)
Delta Force (U.S. Army)
Hostage Rescue Unit (HRU)
SEAL Team 6 or DevGroup
(Naval Special Warfare
Development Group, U.S. Navy)

Text-Dependent Questions

1. Why have there been fewer hijackings since 2001?
2. What was significant about the El Al hijacking incident of 1968?
3. What year were the first U.S. Sky Marshals sworn in?

Research Projects

1. Research the cockpit security measures added after 9/11.
2. What special security measures has Israel pioneered?

A senior USAF airman trains with Italian counterparts to meet high-risk operations.

Series Glosssary

Air marshal: Armed guard traveling on an aircraft to protect the passengers and crew; the air marshal is often disguised as a passenger.

Annexation: To incorporate a country or other territory within the domain of a state.

Armory: A supply of arms for defense or attack.

Assassinate: To murder by sudden or secret attack, usually for impersonal reasons.

Ballistic: Of or relating to firearms.

Biological warfare: Also known as germ warfare, this is war fought with biotoxins—harmful bacteria or viruses that are artificially propagated and deliberately dispersed to spread sickness among an enemy.

Cartel: A combination of groups with a common action or goal.

Chemical warfare: The use of poisonous or corrosive substances to kill or incapacitate the enemy; it differs from biological warfare in that the chemicals concerned are not organic, living germs.

Cold War: A long and bitter enmity between the United States and the Free World and the Soviet Union and its Communist satellites, which went on from 1945 to the collapse of Communism in 1989.

Communism: A system of government in which a single authoritarian party controls state-owned means of production.

Conscription: Compulsory enrollment of persons especially for military service.

Consignment: A shipment of goods or weapons.

Contingency operations: Operations of a short duration and most often performed at short notice, such as dropping supplies into a combat zone.

Counterintelligence: Activities designed to collect information about enemy espionage and then to thwart it.

Covert operations: Secret plans and activities carried out by spies and their agencies.

Cyberterrorism: A form of terrorism that seeks to cause disruption by interfering with computer networks.

Democracy: A government elected to rule by the majority of a country's people.

Depleted uranium: One of the hardest known substances, it has most of its radioactivity removed before being used to make bullets.

Dissident: A person who disagrees with an established religious or political system, organization, or belief.

Embargo: A legal prohibition on commerce.

Emigration: To leave one country to move to another country.

Extortion: The act of obtaining money or other property from a person by means of force or intimidation.

Extradite: To surrender an alleged criminal from one state or nation to another having jurisdiction to try the charge.

Federalize/federalization: The process by which National Guard units, under state command in normal circumstances, are called up by the president in times of crisis to serve the federal government of the United States as a whole.

Genocide: The deliberate and systematic destruction of a racial, political, or cultural group.

Guerrilla: A person who engages in irregular warfare, especially as a member of an independent unit carrying out harassment and sabotage.

Hijack: To take unlawful control of a ship, train, aircraft, or other form of transport.

Immigration: The movement of a person or people ("immigrants") into a country; as opposed to emigration, their movement out.

Indict: To charge with a crime by the finding or presentment of a jury (as a grand jury) in due form of law.

Infiltrate: To penetrate an organization, like a terrorist network.

Infrastructure: The crucial networks of a nation, such as transportation and communication, and also including government organizations, factories, and schools.

Insertion: Getting into a place where hostages are being held.

Insurgent: A person who revolts against civil authority or an established government.

Internment: To hold someone, especially an immigrant, while his or her application for residence is being processed.

Logistics: The aspect of military science dealing with the procurement, maintenance, and transportation of military matériel, facilities, and personnel.

Matériel: Equipment, apparatus, and supplies used by an organization or institution.

Militant: Having a combative or aggressive attitude.

Militia: a military force raised from civilians, which supports a regular army in times of war.

Narcoterrorism: Outrages arranged by drug trafficking gangs to destabilize government, thus weakening law enforcement and creating conditions for the conduct of their illegal business.

NATO: North Atlantic Treaty Organization; an organization of North American and European countries formed in 1949 to protect one another against possible Soviet aggression.

Naturalization: The process by which a foreigner is officially "naturalized," or accepted as a U.S. citizen.

Nonstate actor: A terrorist who does not have official government support.

Ordnance: Military supplies, including weapons, ammunition, combat vehicles, and maintenance tools and equipment.

Refugee: A person forced to take refuge in a country not his or her own, displaced by war or political instability at home.

Rogue state: A country, such as Iraq or North Korea, that ignores the conventions and laws set by the international community; rogue states often pose a threat, either through direct military action or by harboring terrorists.

Sortie: One mission or attack by a single plane.

Sting: A plan implemented by undercover police in order to trap criminals.

Surveillance: To closely watch over and monitor situations; the USAF employs many different kinds of surveillance equipment and techniques in its role as an intelligence gatherer.

Truce: A suspension of fighting by agreement of opposing forces.

UN: United Nations; an international organization, of which the United States is a member, that was established in 1945 to promote international peace and security.

Chronology

1193–1194: King Richard I (Richard the Lionheart) is held hostage for ransom by Duke Leopold of Austria.

1931: February 21, first known aircraft hijacking in Peru; one hostage taken.

1932: Kidnap and murder of the baby son of Charles Lindbergh, the first man to fly alone across the Atlantic in 1927.

1968: Hijacking of an El Al aircraft by the Popular Front for the Liberation of Palestine; the 32 passengers on board are held for five weeks before being freed; the hijackers escape.

1970: Canadian government minister Pierre Laporte is kidnapped and murdered.

1976: Israeli special forces rescue 101 Israeli and Jewish hostages held at Entebbe Airport, Uganda, by terrorists in the name of the Palestine Liberation Organization (PLO).

1977: South Moluccan terrorists hijack a train in the Netherlands and hold 94 passengers hostage for three weeks.

1978: Kidnapping and murder of Aldo Moro, Italian presidential candidate.

1980: SAS rescues hostages from the Iranian Embassy, London; the rescue is covered live on international television.

1983: FBI's Hostage Rescue Team is formed.

1985: Italian cruise liner *Achille Lauro*, with 454 passengers and crew on board, is seized by four terrorists; one hostage is murdered; two of the terrorists are later put on trial and imprisoned; the other two are freed.

1987: Terry Waite, special representative of the Archbishop of Canterbury, England, negotiates the release of many hostages taken by terrorists in Lebanon; but in January of the same year, Waite is himself taken hostage and not released until November 1991.

1987: The FBI's Hostage Rescue Team helps to free 124 hostages taken by inmates at Atlanta Prison, USA.

1993: The FBI's Hostage Rescue Team is involved in the siege of the Branch Davidian religious group at Waco, TX, who held children as hostages; the siege ended in a fire in which 87 people, including 17 children, died.

1996: December 17, the Japanese ambassador's home in Lima, Peru, is surrounded by Marxist rebels, who take the 600 party guests hostage; the last 74 hostages are not rescued until April 1997.

2013: Alabama bunker hostage crisis; Jimmy Lee Dykes kidnaps a 5-year-old boy from a school bus in Alabama, killing the bus driver. Three HRT team members rescue the boy. Dykes is killed during the rescue.

2013: HRT rescues a teenager, killing the person who abducted her.

2014: HRT rescues Frank Arthur Janssen in North Carolina after he was held for five days by people wanting the release of an inmate at Polk Correctional Institution.

2016: HRT are part of the confrontation with militants occupying Malheur National Wildlife Refuge in Oregon.

Further Resources

Websites

History of the SAS: www.guardian.co.uk/waronteror/story

Information about Delta Force (U.S. Army): www.specialforces.net/Delta_Force

The Israeli raid on Entebbe (Uganda) in 1976: www.claremont.org/precepts

Rescue One SWAT (police): rescuel.com/swat6.htm

FBI Hostage Rescue Team (HRT): www.specialoperations.com

The FBI Hostage Rescue Team: www.fbi.gov/video-repository/newss-hostage-rescue-team-marks-30-years/view

Federal Bureau of Investigation (FBI) Special Operations and Response Units; Hostage Rescue Team (HRT); Critical Incident Response Group (CIRG); The FBI's Critical Incident Response Group (CIRG): www.specialoperations.com/Domestic/FBI

The Navy SEALs, Army Rangers, and the Army's SFOD-Delta (Delta Force): www.geocities.com

Counterterrorism guide page: www.angelfire.com/nt/tic6/strategys/strategyscscom

Counterterrorist groups of the world: www.specwarnet.com

Further Reading

Coulson, Danny O. and Elaine Shannon. *No Heroes: Inside the FBI's Secret Counter-terror Force.* New York: Pocket Books, 1999.

McNab, Chris. *Hostage Rescue with the SAS. Elite Forces, Survival Guides.* Philadelphia: Mason Crest, 2002.

Thompson, Leroy. *Hostage Rescue Manual.* London: Greenhill Books, 2001.

Whitcombe, Christopher. *Cold Zero: Inside the FBI Hostage Rescue Team.* Boston: Little, Brown, 2001.

Whiting, Jim. *U.S. Special Forces: FBI Hostage Rescue & SWAT Teams.* Mankato, MN: Creative Paperbacks, 2015.

Index

About the Author

Brenda Ralph Lewis is a prolific writer of books, articles, television documentary scripts, and other materials on history, royalty, military subjects, aviation, and philately. Her writing includes many books on ancient history, culture, and life; and books on World War II, including *The Hitler Youth: The Hitlerjugend in Peace and War 1933–1945* (2000), *Women At War* (2001), and *The Story of Anne Frank* (2001). She has also written or contributed to numerous books for children, including The Aztecs (1999), *Stamps! A Young Philatelist's Guide* (1998), and *Ritual Sacrifice: A History* (2002). She lives in Buckinghamshire, England.

About the Consultant

Manny Gomez, an expert on terrorism and security, is President of MG Security Services and a former Principal Relief Supervisor and Special Agent with the FBI. He investigated terrorism and espionage cases as an agent in the National Security Division. He was a certified undercover agent and successfully completed Agent Survival School. Chairman of the Board of the National Law Enforcement Association (NLEA), Manny is also a former Sergeant in the New York Police Department (NYPD) where he supervised patrol and investigative activities of numerous police officers, detectives and civilian personnel. Mr. Gomez worked as a uniformed and plainclothes officer in combating narcotics trafficking, violent crimes, and quality of life concerns. He has executed over 100 arrests and received Departmental recognition on eight separate occasions. Mr. Gomez has a Bachelor's Degree and Master's Degree and is a graduate of Fordham University School of Law where he was on the Dean's list. He is admitted to the New York and New Jersey Bar. He served honorably in the United States Marine Corps infantry.